Untold Evidence of God

By

Andre Dell'Erba

Copyright © 2010 by Andre Dell'Erba

Untold Evidence of God
by Andre Dell'Erba

Printed in the United States of America

ISBN 9781609571320

All rights reserved solely by the author. The author guarantees all contents are original and do not infringe upon the legal rights of any other person or work. No part of this book may be reproduced in any form without the permission of the author. The views expressed in this book are not necessarily those of the publisher.

Unless otherwise indicated, Bible quotations are taken from The New King James Version. Copyright © 1982 by Thomas Nelson, Inc.

www.xulonpress.com

CONTENT

Chapter 1 – WHY is this important? 7

Chapter 2 – The Designer, Creator OR "Lucky" Chaos? 14
   i)   What about the Theory of Evolution? 15

Chapter 3 – EVIDENCE of the Designer through hard science 21
   i)   Cambrian age, Creation of life ("supposedly" 543-490 Million years) 22
   ii) Humans vs. Animals 27
   iii) Bacteria Flagellum motor 29
   iv) DNA (Deoxyribo Nucleic Acid) 30
   v) Chromosomes 33
   vi) Population Projections 35
   vii) No such thing as truly "physical" 37
   viii) What is the meaning of life? 39

Chapter 4 - Want to SEE God?................................47

Chapter 5 – Have you challenged your base?........55

Chapter 6 - Is the Bible LITERALLY God's Word?....58
    i)   Any ancient historical sources saying the same thing?..59
    ii) What are the amazing facts?......................61
    iii) How do we know man didn't write the Bible to keep peace? 67
    iv) What are the main messages and themes in the Bible?...................................70
    v) How do we know the writers were inspired by God? 76

Chapter 7 - Is Jesus the Messiah, the One we are to SURRENDER to? 90

Chapter 1

WHY is this important?

Today, tomorrow, the day after and then what? We gather, we heap up, we strive for perfection... for what? What happens if we receive everything, then what, what comes next? And does it truly make a difference? Can life be lived without the mortal end in mind, knocked to and fro without thought until we die? This life being a matter of chance; some big random event that took place in a period of time through disorganized chaos? Or was it designed with the purpose of weeding out the rebellious hearts?

I'm not a debater, nor an intellectual, nor a scientist, nor a philosopher, nor religious. I am just one who thinks twice, a member of Mensa, who spent and still spends much time in the sciences. I have recently been asked to "Prove God logically" and my response is "That's easy."

Now if I had been asked to "prove God didn't exist logically" that would be difficult because I would be forced to ignore hard facts and focus on soft theories, like the theory of Evolution or the Theory of Self-Reliance. I once believed in these theories wholeheartedly, even professed them as truth until I started questioning them. As I grew in my understanding and research I realized that these theories are weak and that it takes far more faith and convincing to believe them, than believing that life was purposely designed and created.

I am very disappointed in the way the educational system has taught on the subject of evolution. How unsupported facts and biased data were taught to me as facts. Now they either didn't know about the zero foundation on which the Theory of Evolution stands and were just a product of the education system like me, or they had a hidden agenda which wasn't about science but about "removing

God". People holding to this Theory come out with statements like "God vs. Science", where it should have been "Science vs. Science".

The Theory of Evolution seemed like it initially started off as a scientific theory but when discoveries were made in the 60-90's, contrary to the Theory, they weren't publicized and didn't make it into the education system. And when "some" of this data was shared by scientists they were labelled as "Religious Fundamentalists" and ridiculed. Since the mass had already been brainwashed and adopted the Theory of Evolution as the answer to life, or the lack thereof, people didn't challenge science or the data that led to the theory. If science is about facts why hide the evidence – I will touch on this shortly.

I remember one afternoon when I was young, less than 10 years old; my parents' friends came over for a barbecue. I was bored with adult company so I decided to play with the new sand my father had bought for the recently laid grass. After playing with the sand I went inside to see if the food was ready. To my amazement everyone was in the same position as when I left, except my father who was turning the meat. On the way back to the pile of sand I stopped, turned around at the top of the driveway and asked myself, "Do people move only when I am in their presence, or do they stop moving when I'm not there? Are they just puppets for me? Why am I here? And why am I me? Do I belong to myself? Who made me; I know I didn't make myself? Without me, will this sand have any meaning (significance)?" It was like I had been programmed with this quest, a natural hunger that came from my inner most being. It was like I was created to know the answer, not kill the desire. It was as if someone was calling me to know.

Later, I realized that all have had similar questions at some point in their life. As if we were programmed to find it. Some ended at the Theory of Evolution, Theory of Self-reliance, Idols that they make, an impersonal force, and others ended at an intelligent personal Creator. Who is correct? Or maybe that isn't the right question – the question should be what is the answer irrespective of who we believe is correct?

Now the older I became, the wiser I thought myself to be. Science and those who taught science started playing a larger role in my life. I became a 'God' sceptic. If someone gave me one reason why God existed, I could give them 1,000 reasons why He didn't. Like most people today; it is all a façade based on false presumptions. My standard answer was founded on the Theory of Evolution which I believed to be true – taught to be true. And I could put people in a scientific head spin with masses of data and assumptions. I portrayed having all the answers with "science" but deep down I had more questions than answers, which made me feel hypocritical and empty at times. As I went deeper into the Theory of Evolution – I started asking myself "Why do I believe this garbage, when the data, and the fact that we are interpreting the data, points to a Designer/Creator?"

This Theory of Evolution literally had no foundation and yet I had built a tower on it, which would not and could not sustain me because it couldn't sustain itself. Even if I take garbage and wrap it in a scientific wrapper, with lights, bells and whistles, it is still garbage. So why was there a tendency to sway from an intelligent personal Designer behind creation? Was it because I wanted to be accountable to myself? Maybe. Was it that I considered myself intelligent and therefore if I believed there was a Designer, Creator, I wouldn't be intelligent and would be ridiculed, and labelled as a "Religious Fundamentalist"?

Through the next few pages, I will take you on my journey of peeling back the onion to the obvious truth. So the stench of the obvious heart of truth may come to the surface. It isn't rocket science, just simple reasoning. It is the power of thinking beyond what we have been taught or influenced - The power of thinking twice about life. It is important to question our beliefs to all limits, and assess if they are sustainable or if we can sustain ourselves. If not, why do we rest on this?

Why is this important? Our words and actions come from our thoughts; and every thought is governed by our set of beliefs; and every belief we have is established by an authority we choose. This is the foundation of our decisions. The authority can either be a legitimate authority or not, but we end up choosing the authority and live by the consequences or benefits of the choices we make based on that authority. Who is your authority – God, Self or Another?

At the end of peeling back the onion on life I came to realize, that just like gravity, whether I choose to believe that gravity exists or not, it has no effect on the fact that it exists, and I reap the consequences every time I act contrary. Whether I know about it or not it makes no difference. Similarly with God (the Creator), whether I believe God exists or not, it doesn't change the fact that He is and that He will hold me accountable for the choices I make. And every time I act contrary, I reap the consequences, which may not be instant but are eventually reaped.

"For since the creation of the world His invisible attributes are clearly seen, being understood by the things that are made, even His eternal power and Godhead, so that they are without excuse, because, although they knew God, they did not glorify Him as God, nor were thankful, but became futile in their thoughts, and their foolish hearts were darkened. Professing to be wise, they became fools" (Romans 1:20-22).

Chapter 2

The Designer, Creator OR "Lucky" Chaos?

Is there such a thing as random or chaos? Is random like throwing dice and chaos like breaking glass? Both are governed by forces that are initiated by "someone" (the initiator). Also someone had to create what "force is" and "how it" operates in the first place (Designer, Creator). If this isn't established then there is no environment through which an initiator can initiate. As in the example of the dice, the initiator throws a dice within an environment which is designed. By understanding the laws that were designed and established in that environment, we can control the dice there in. This will result in us being able to determine where, how and when the dice will land every time; therefore it is no longer random. We know! The number on the dice can be calculated by controlling the starting position; frictional forces of the surface and the dice; the speed and angle of release, travel and rotation in the air and ground; gravity and weight; the temperature and wind; shape of the dice, etc. So what are we saying then? There is no such thing as random, except for a lack of understanding on our part. Lack of understanding of the environment that the Designer created, and how the Initiator (sometimes the Designer, the Environment itself, or someone else) uses that environment.

i)   What about the Theory of Evolution?

It takes far more faith to believe this theory than to believe it was created by the Creator. I'm not just saying this because of a religious persuasion but based on hard science.

The idea that people developed from bacteria/cell billions of years ago - from sludge, to bacteria, to fish, to an ape, to a human may sound logical to some but it sounds crazy to others (literally moving from the goo through the zoo to you). To those that say it is logical – let's play it out. What would happen if I stood up on the street corner and proclaimed that the sludge under my shoe would develop over millions of years into a person like you - would you believe me or laugh at me? What would happen if I showed my hypothesis via a drawing of the development over time - would that change anything? What would happen if I demonstrated that humans can evolve based on the environment e.g. in colder climates getting thicker and more hair - Would that support my initial theory or would that be easily explained away? What would happen if I had some title behind my name that people said made me smarter than you? If I made it more complex by adding a scientific maze of assumptions, would you surrender and default to believing me because it is too complex to cut through yourself?

That's the Theory of Evolution by Darwin "the Origin of Species." It is based on the Theory of Natural Selection driving progressive unintelligent change and development from a single cell to all the species we have today, with no intelligent intervention. Instead of the similarity of physical features pointing to a common Designer, Darwin implied that it was a result of a common starting point. He had very little to say on how the cell started. He never addressed how life started in the cell or how living matter could come from non-living matter (elements and molecules). He never addressed how the environment was established in which the change happened. His primary focus was on the assumption of evolving, that is, comparing species that evolve within species to - one specie evolving into completely different species.

What about "Punctuated Equilibrium"? Punctuated Equilibrium is a theory in evolution that states that most sexually reproducing organisms (genetic diversity of offspring) will show little to no change during history. Punctuated Equilibrium is commonly contrasted against the Theory of Phyletic Gradualism, which "hypothesizes" that most evolution occurs uniformly and gradually over time. Both theories are based on the hypothesis that one changes instantly and the other over time. Again no proof for change of one specie into another. If this was the case, based on these hypotheses, we would have many half-ape half-humans today.

Consider "Genetic Algorithm" - The progression from a specific state (given state) to a better state? The progression is based on looking at the individual members called "candidate solutions" evaluating their fitness and sustainability in that environment (excludes millions of factors) and then taking some members, mutating them (not saying what makes them change but actually changing their coding to produce a better outcome) and then hypothesizing what the end of the generation will look like. This becomes the start of the next generation and a so-called "fact" and so on until the population arrives at the better solution (fabricating the outcome on assumptions).

Hard science is fact based and can be proven and soft science is theory/assumptions, like Evolution. There is no foundation, no natural progression of one specie to the next (species become extinct but do not evolve to another specie), no evidence of evolution in transition, no evidence of the sustainability of evolution, it has no starting point and no end point – basically it is a "Theory of Unintelligent Chaos" which is not and cannot be sustained by hard science.

The theory is only solid if it has a solid foundation. Adversely, a weak foundation results in a weak theory, e.g. the foundation of Evolution is less than weak - From the proposed development of the cell to the mutation through natural selection. Even in Mathematics if we don't have either a solid starting point or an end point as a reference, we can pretty much make up what we want and it doesn't prove anything. In the case of the Theory of Evolution there is neither a starting nor an end point.

Hard Science disproved the Theory of Evolution more than 30 years ago yet it is still being taught in schools as a scientific fact. Why? Because the Theory of Evolution has become "the religion" of the 20th Century to give people like me "an excuse" to side step what hard science points to - the Creator, the Designer. Questioning the Theory of Evolution from a scientific basis undoubtedly causes scientists to be labeled as religious fundamentalists. This may be a "scare tactic" or a method of diversion to sustain the theory and avoid scrutiny. Why? Because the Theory of Evolution uses the excuse "Religious Fundamentalist" to hide the fact that they themselves are "Religious Fundamentalists" pushing an incredible high faith; supposedly under the banner of science.

Some say it isn't a religion - But it is, religion is "seeking after god", and their god(s) is self. It reminds me of the Nazi's and Communist brainwashing in the education system — there is no difference. Their foundation was exactly the same as educators of "Theory of Evolution"– to prove there is "NO" Designer. Just like communism, the Theory of Evolution too will collapse as people take life and hard science seriously.

Chapter 3

EVIDENCE of the Designer through hard science

Now let's talk about the Designer, Creator ... God. Is there any hard proof there is a Designer, a Creator of all? The answer is Life – the ability to reason, to give meaning, love - basically who we are. Life transcends beyond atoms, molecules, electrons or elements – these express life but don't create it. For we didn't decide to be born, or where to be born, nor from whom to be born; nor did we decide to love; nor did we develop or decide what is truly good and evil; nor did we decide what laws govern life and nature; nor did we create the earth, life on it and the principles by which it operates; nor do we have the ability to live forever or raise ourselves from the dead; nor did we create what is after death and the rules to get there. So what is it that we truly own? Just one thing - Choice.

A choice that has been given to us – embedded in us to reason in order to produce love. Life gives us the ability to reason beyond what we see, governing life based on "good" and "evil." We do this through the foundation we all live by - love. Again no atoms, electrons, molecules or element creates this. Life in itself is the very proof that a Personal God created us and everything around us.

Now let's talk about life. Hard/factual Science always opposes Chaos/Evolution and points to the Creator/Designer:

i) Cambrian age, Creation of life ("supposedly" 543-490 Million years)

This is an age explained in archaeology at the very beginning where life forms/ species started – the explosion of life. There isn't an age of living organisms/fossils before this age. The Precambrian age – people have believed there were "non complex" life forms like bacteria during this age in order to support the Theory of Evolution but they have no proof. Based on archaeological findings, all species <u>existed at once</u> and they <u>didn't develop over</u> millions and millions of years with slow progression, as the Theory of Evolution states. However, change within species is possible but not from one specie to another. The Cambrian age does not include human beings existing during this time, but at the same time it does not negate that it could or the possibility of later introduction.

Some Evolutionists have argued that fossil preservation was not possible owing to the small and soft bodies of life forms. People have believed this argument for years. However, over the last 20 years, archaeologists in China have found sponge embryos dating as far back as the Cambrian age – soft and microscopic. If they can find a sponge that doesn't have bones, surely they can find progression of life forms. None have been found to date, none to support the Theory of Evolution.

Soft science, with the assumption based on various dating methods, says there were Ice Ages or an

Ice Age. An Ice Age is a general term used for Glaciers covering the earth. The Ice Age was split into 4 major time periods, apparently 800 to 600 million years ago, 460 to 430 million years ago, 350 to 250 million years ago and the last one was 4 million years ago, with the earth's age projecting to ~4,500 million years ago.

So what about the accuracy of dating methods used to predict the age of something? If using dating with other historical facts then it is pretty accurate. But pure dating is not accurate – not even 80/20. The depletion of the dating element takes place over thousands of years. Scientists have assumed how long it depletes based on a particular environment. If the environment changes then the depletion rate changes, also it is not linear and not exponential. No one can time the actual length of the depletion from beginning to end, so they measure it over a fraction of time and then extrapolate it over its life.

For example; apparently the half life of Carbon is 5,700 years and reliable for dating up to 60,000 years. This cannot be measured in full, only a fraction of it. At best 0.1% of the time frame, it is then extrapolated. This ignores environmental factors.

It is like taking your pulse over 1 second and then saying, "Your average pulse for your entire life will be ... And you will live for ..." What happens if your fitness changes, or your environment changes, or your body changes? Your pulse will change accordingly. One second is far too short to make an accurate assessment for a life assumption; the same inaccuracy applies to dating.

Before negating what the Bible says about the origin of life, let's take another look. God created the heavens and the earth (Gen. 1:1). The scripture doesn't say when exactly the heavens and the earth were created. It could be 7,000 to Billions of years ago. However it does talk about a Pre-Adamic world, a world that existed before Adam and Eve, i.e. before the first humans.

There were intelligent beings, non-human, who had choice/freewill to choose God. They were under the rule of an Angelic being called Lucifer (Ezek. 28:12-16; Is. 14:4-6, 9-12). There was one world order. This was probably the time when dinosaurs like the T-Rex roamed the earth. Lucifer elevated himself as god and led those beings astray to worship him, just like many do today (Is. 14:12-15; Ezek. 28:12-19; Luke 10:18). As a result God judged him and them. He stripped Lucifer of the authority and cast him down to the earth (Luke 10:18). God removed His light from the earth and flooded it with water – this resulted in the earth being in a destructive state, like a ball of ice (Gen. 1:2; Jer. 4:23-26; Job 9:5-9; 26:5-13; 38:28-33).

God reconstructed the earth and then created Adam and Eve, the first humans – all within six literal days not millions of years (Gen. 1:3-28). This was about 6,000 years ago. At this time the earth was at most part one unit. Then God judged the world again and flooded it, saving Noah and his family (3 sons and their wives). Then after the flood the earth started splitting apart (1 Chr. 1:19). God spoke about these in His Word before anyone knew that the earth was one and had been split apart. It didn't take millions of years as soft science claims – also these theories are assumptions based on how the earth is drifting apart today, add a few big earthquakes and the entire calculation drastically speeds up.

What about the different ethnic groups? Hard science tells us that we adapt to our environment not that we evolve into another specie to meet that environment. The Bible talks about the colour of skin changing based on the environment, e.g. Job was from the region of Arabia and his skin became black based on the environment and the situation he was in (Job 30:30). Adapting to one's environment, within the parameters of the specie, is part of the design God created. For example if your ancestors and you spent most of your time in the water, you will not develop gills or turn into a fish. I guarantee you this. However your skin will change to help accommodate the impact of the water, yet you will still be a human.

ii) Humans vs. Animals

Aren't humans the same as animals? I have to say that some animals behave better than some humans, yet they both have the same Creator, but irrespective they are different at the very core of their life i.e. Choice/Free-will vs. Instinct. Humans have been given the intellectual ability to choose to act contrary to creation and the Creator. No animal comes close to possessing the reasoning ability God gave humans. An animal will not change its authority on which it basis its decisions unless its environment changes. However a human has the ability to change their beliefs irrespective of the environment.

So the fundamental difference is that humans can choose to serve God or not. This is the choice that God has given them. Animals cannot choose God but live by Him and are influenced by humans. Therefore it is true that the reason humans behave like animals is because they haven't chosen the Creator as their authority and therefore when they act contrary to Him, knowingly or unknowingly, there are consequences experienced by creation, self and others. When a human doesn't choose God as their authority they end up being worse off than animals because they have no way of knowing what is true and the impact they generate is far worse. As the Bible says, "A fool says in his heart there is no God" (Ps. 53:1).

iii) Bacteria Flagellum motor

The very cell isn't life or the source of life but it contains life. The cell is a house, a vehicle for life to express itself. A cell is like a car and the driver is the life. Without a clear understanding of the cell there is no way we can understand its change. The Theory of Evolution refers to natural selection being the primary mutation force for the development/mutation of the cells. However the cell doesn't operate like this. The bacterial flagellum motor is an integral part within the cell which helps the cell move. The Bacterial flagellum motor houses an intelligent agent that enables it to reason - called life. It looks like a speedboat motor and by looking at it you will realize that it cannot be built gradually or built based on natural selection but by a designer. It requires all of its parts simultaneously to function. If one of the ~40 protein parts is missing, it will not work and the life will not work through it.

The Theory of Evolution, through natural selection, renders each of the 40 protein parts independently useless until they come together, hence no motor would have been developed using natural selection. And this is where the Theory of Natural Selection implodes on itself, at the very core of living matter - the cell. If the smallest component doesn't operate according to the principle of natural selection how can the entire unit operate in the same way! It is like taking all the units of a wristwatch. Each unit is designed for a specific purpose. Then putting them in your pocket, swinging then around in different environments for millions of years and then it turns into a working grandfather clock. This may sound ridiculous but this is exactly what the Theory of Evolution expects people to believe. And many fall for it through the confusion of so called intellect.

The Bacteria Flagellum motor itself (the way it looks) and how it operates (the life within giving the ability to reason), proves that there is a Designer/Creator who designed, created and provided specific DNA coding for it to multiply.

iv)   DNA (Deoxyribo Nucleic Acid)

DNA is the coding information to build a specific part of the body. The genome is "all" the DNA in an organism, including its genes. Genes carry information for making all the proteins required by all organisms. These proteins determine, among other things, how the organism looks, how well its body metabolizes food or fights infection, and sometimes even how it behaves. All species have different DNA. Without DNA no cell replication can take place. It tells the cells what to do.

The protein components that make up the structure are made, shaped and organized by coding called DNA. DNA is found within the nucleus. The protein is created with precision - perfect size, perfect shape and perfect sequence. Then and only then can it be useful. Protein (more specifically amino acids) coming together randomly i.e. "the Theory of Chemical Evolution" is not possible and was rejected more than 20 years ago by science. They discovered that a protein unit cannot come together without the specific sequencing program called DNA (who do you think provided this program?). It is infinitely easier to take 1,000,000 coins of the same size, randomly throw them down on a flat surface hoping they will ALL land on top of each other, in the right sequence, than to get the coding right by chance.

Let's hypothesize that archaeologists find an airport covered in sand and ice. They estimate it is 1,000 million years old. The planes on the runway are frozen in time. Each plane has a very complex electrical circuitry connecting the engines and the navigation system to the main airport tower. Within this there is specific coding. They speculate that the airport and planes evolved out of the trees, rocks and rivers over millions and billions of years. It became so advanced that this airport reproduced itself to other parts of this world. Would you believe this? It seems highly improbable that anyone would believe it. Yet many believe DNA coding happened by chance.

DNA can be compared to an advanced computer language – Designers establish a code and write the program to read the code. The operators use the computer which activates the program and code. The operators are the cells which are governed by life. They use the DNA (code) to express life (program) that was intended by the Creator. DNA provides specific genetic instruction to build one protein within the simplest cell. This coding would fill hundreds and thousands of printed texts in programming. The instructions for the forces required in each amino exchange would fill many more pages than the DNA coding and sequencing. It is only logical to assume that this information was coded and built by the Creator (God).

v) Chromosomes

Some Evolutionists, such as I once was, have argued humans and great apes (gorilla's not chimps) have similar chromosomes; i.e. Humans (23 pairs) and great Apes (24 pairs). They hypothesize that at one point there could have been "a fusion event" for the 24 pairs to become 23. Not even in a lab with human intervention can they make this happen and then have a cell survive. And when you add up all the so called "small differences" which aren't small (like Chromosomes, DNA, Reasoning against creation), you end up with a completely different specie, as it was designed. It is like looking at two sets of gears, one for a bicycle and one for a car, they are both made from metal, they both have gears arranged in a circular pattern and then we hypothesize they are for the same vehicle or somehow one was changed by an event. However there are so many differences besides just the gears that when you add them up

– it is innumerable. A human is far more complex than any car or bicycle.

The impossibility is scientifically astounding but to add to this impossibility of Evolution, not just one ape became a human through cell change but two apes – and more specifically making one male and one female human. And to add to this impossibility, they both changed at the same time in order to exist e.g. A human male having sex with a female ape, or vice versa, can't procreate – hard science tells you this. Do you know the impossibility of all these things taking place? It is far more realistic that Adam and Eve were created by God and populated the earth than this theory.

Even within the coding and sequencing, females have two of the same gender chromosomes (XX) and males have two distinct gender chromosomes (XY). Males and females are different but compatible yet not compatible across species. Now when scientists trace the ancestry, they use the Y – the male chromosome (haplogroup). They say it goes back to two humans – a male and a female. There is no ancestry traced to apes, because that's when hard science changes to soft science (assumptions and hypothesis). Isn't it amazing that the Bible has been saying for thousands of years that the population came from two people – literally Adam and Eve, and now ancestral tracing confirms this!

vi) Population Projections

Based on the Theory of Evolution hypothesis, humans have been around for millions of years. And based on the Bible, they have been around for ~6,000 years (since Adam and Eve). Which one is more correct; ~6000 or millions of years? Based on mathematics and history of child births, wars, disasters and famine; 6000-4500 years is the most probable to get us to the population we have today ~6,7 Billion people on earth.

However being true to scripture, ~1,500 years after the start from Adam and Eve, the entire world was flooded by God, and the re-population started again with Noah's 3 Sons and their wives (~4,500 years ago). So let's look at a very conservative logical calculation for population, with this starting point ~4,500 years. Let's say

- 40% of the population is eliminated every 500 years due to famines, wars and disasters (very conservative number, historically this was less as the disasters were concentrated in certain areas and not always a global impact).

- The average life span of a person was ~ 45 years old (also very conservative, historically it is between 50-60years).

Based on the above criteria, what would the population rate be for a couple in order to have 6.7 billion people, as today? ~2.3 children per couple – very feasible, this is a conservative number and this was before the 20th century contraception period. If we say it was millions of years, then the population rate per couple is basically flat (historically, on a macro level this was not true) as families had many children, cases of 10-15 children weren't uncommon for a wife. Children were a sign of prosperity and blessings in most cultures of the world. Also many men had more than one wife/concubine who had children, thus increasing the ratio even further. Another fact that goes against the millions of years is – "what disaster/war killed so many" (that's when you see assumptions come in that can't be substantiated historically and yet assured to be true). Thus the 2.3 children per couple is a conservative number and lines up with the Bible. Humans are not 200million years old as Evolution believes but 6,000 years old.

vii) No such thing as truly "physical"

The physical is made up of the non-physical. And it is life that gives meaning, reasoning, expression to the physical. Without life, there is no meaning, no reasoning, no expression – nothing. Hard science tells us that all matter is made up of variations of energy and there is nothing actually solid. Matter can be broken down into elements/atoms (e.g. Hydrogen, Iron, Carbon etc.), the higher the energy holding the elements together the harder the matter. The element itself can be broken down further, into the Nucleus and Electrons, again held together by even higher energy.

The Nucleus can be broken down further into Protons and Neutrons, again held together by more energy. Each can be broken down further again. A Proton can be broken down into Quarks held together by even more intense energy. A Quark itself can be broken down further into Pre-ions again held together by even more intense energy, and so on, and so on.

Nothing is solid and all physical is just a variation of energy – some more intense than others. So why do we stop at the physical or use the physical to explain the physical as people try to do with the Big Bang Theory – trying to use a rock to explain life? You laugh but this is the big bang theory – it uses non life things to explain life. It ignores life altogether (the ability to reason against creation and reason meaning), and the laws that govern life and energy. Both of these need to be actually created and parameters established for it to work together in harmony. So using Theories only based on the Physical ignores the foundation, the non physical. And the non physical points you to energy and the life that gives the energy meaning. And this points to the Creator and Sustainer and Giver of life - God. You don't have to be a genius to figure this out. Sometimes I feel like the boy in the Emperor's new clothes - pointing out the obvious.

viii)   What is the meaning of life?

Many have said they bank their life on hard facts, science, things that can be proven by science but this is not true. Everyone bases their life on their own meaning and ethics. There is no science course proving meaning or proving ethics but yet this is what governs their decisions. So what is the meaning of life? Some say happiness, but what is happiness except an output of meaning, output of purpose. No hard science can prove meaning of life because meaning transcends beyond the borders of matter.

Is energy life? No, we know from hard science that energy doesn't reason on its own, it doesn't have intellect, it doesn't have love, doesn't work by faith. So what gives energy an expression, the ability to act on the reasoning? LIFE. It is life within the energy that does all of this. Without life, energy would be meaningless, pointless because life gives energy meaning. Life isn't energy but life is reasoning, the ability to make choices. For humans, it is the ability to reason outside of what we see and the ability to think about meaning.

Think about this - We can take most of the body parts out and keep the body functioning by pumping the blood and providing oxygen; trying to make the environment satisfactory for life (the ability to reason) to stay. But when the life leaves then the ability to reason has gone. They measure life activity (reasoning activity) through brainwaves. The brain doesn't give the life but it is a vehicle through which the life tells the body how to operate. The body is a house of energy that expresses life. When the energy environment (body) isn't satisfactory, the life (reasoning, intellect, choices, emotions, character - us) leaves. Life is who we are, we are not the energy house (the body) but the life in the energy house.

So what is life's primary motive? To bear fruit. Everything that has life bears fruit and there is a primary fruit for all life. A fruit tree gives shade but its primary motive is to bear fruit. An animal is part of the ecosystem but its primary motive is to procreate. For humans it is also to procreate but our primary motive is to produce LOVE. Love is the foundation of human decisions. If a person doesn't have love they self destruct. It is love which is the primary motive, not food, not shelter, love is the strongest.

It is only possible to love when tapped into the One who designed us to love – God.

The question that will be asked is - if God wants us to love why did He create suffering, He doesn't seem like a God of love? Let's talk about you first and then we will answer the question concerning God. What gives you the right to bring accusations against the Designer, did you create yourself, are you self righteous? What are you doing with your time to alleviate those who are suffering? Or are you just a finger pointer and not an agent that God wants to use to help those in need? Most people who ask this question do nothing to help those in need, or help just enough to justify themselves. Are you justifying your lack of responsibility by accusing God? This world is not governed by God but by the people. It is God who has given them dominion and authority over the earth (Gen. 1:28) – why do you think Jesus told us to pray that God's Will be done on earth as it is in Heaven? Because it isn't always being done on earth. God isn't sending people to Hell; they are choosing to go by choosing themselves over Him.

But in answer to the original question – "If God wants us to love why did He create suffering? Would you know what love and joy is without suffering? Can there be compassion without suffering? Happiness without Sadness? Good without Evil? Could you really have the correct choices without the consequences to navigate you? Again proving the law of absolute truth is vital for human survival. How would you navigate what is right without suffering? Being told not to? Come on. If I jump off a building and didn't hurt myself, I would do it again even if people told me I shouldn't. But if there was pain, well, then that would be another story.

All suffering is a by-product of our rebellion against God and His creation, and yes many times the innocent suffer. Like abortions – millions of children are killed because we think we know best, no disaster or disease in history has killed more than this and yet we think we are righteous? Much of the world's suffering comes from the people who believe them self to be God, thus making the wrong choices and negate life.

Love is the foundation, and God created us to love. To love who, what? 1) To love the Creator (God) above our self, 2) to love our self and 3) to love others like our self – this is man's all. Why do you think people have a deep satisfaction in helping others because this is what they have been designed to do by the Creator. But it is impossible to love self and others if God isn't our first love. Without God being the primary source of our love we place ourselves above others, i.e. going against God's design. This results in our lack of value for life. Our value shifts to our self, specifically our conveniences and what we decide is right. Success is measured in having money and lots of it, and many follow those who have money as if they have the answers to life. Accountability to self alone results in acting like the Nazi's, the abortion clinics and many other examples of people placing more importance on their convenience, their lifestyle, than life. This rebellion against the Creator and His design results in bad fruit, superficial love. Therefore only when we love God, then we value life and put the value in its true order – God, self and others like self.

So the true meaning of life is intimacy/communion with the Author of love, God. But our rebellion gets in the way and we can never meet God's standards. So God sent His only Son, Jesus Christ, to bridge the gap between God and man – this is true peace. His Son showed us the way to love sacrificially and to BE the way. And when we accept Him as our Owner (it is our Choice), we will follow His example and live BY Him. Because He lives we live. His fruit of love is made manifest in and through us. This results in us automatically loving Him, loving self and loving others, as per the Designer's design.

It is no coincidence that it was Christians who started hospitals, who started orphanages, who started feeding those starving in Africa, who started organizations to help protect and feed children like World Vision, who started the schools for the handicapped, and who consistently out give non-Christians 10 to 1 (look at the government records), and who will sacrifice themselves to go to hostile areas to teach God's love through missions. Many giving up their lives sacrificially to help those who kill them – even today. What about "the crusades"? Not everyone who says they follow Christ does. If you want to see a true Christian – look at Jesus Christ and what He taught.

There is and was no one on earth who has made a bigger impact in the area of love than Jesus Christ. People follow heroes, but who can compare to the greatest hero, Jesus Christ. And He professed to be the Son of God and the only way to God. The question is - do you believe Him, or not? And a bigger question, do you want to know? Or is it a question of your intellect and achievements vs. His? The evidence speaks if you truly seek to know.

His Word is truth – which is contained in the Bible. The Bible comprises of books which are inspired by God. He tells us how to love and be love to others. You may not believe the Bible, perhaps you believe it is written by man. But irrespective, you can't ignore that there is no other book that comes close to the area of love, justice, mercy, truth, accuracy, impact, and power than the Bible. And when countries or people implement His Word, good things happen. Do you think it is a coincidence that less than 5% of the world's population controls the rest? Or that the Biblical prophecies concerning the rise and fall of

Israel are a coincidence? Or that only 7 evil empires would govern God's people throughout history, just 1 left? Or that the signs of the Messiah are fulfilled in Jesus Christ? Coincidence? I will provide these hard facts shortly.

Chapter 4

Want to SEE God?

Y ou can through the eyes of logic. Some who don't really want to know if there is a Creator make statements like, "I can't see Him therefore He is not there? Or how can you believe if you cannot see God, isn't this in your mind?" That's logical! It is like saying I don't see electricity therefore it doesn't exist, it's in my mind. Or I don't see the wind therefore it doesn't exist, it's in my mind. Or I don't see gravity therefore it doesn't exist, it's in my mind. Or what about something that is personal – I don't see love or reasoning or your brain therefore it doesn't exist. The very air we breathe, the food we eat, the ground we are standing on, the body we are in, was given to us by the Creator. Are we like unthankful fish in a tank who don't know that someone put them there, and keeps feeding them?

Scientifically the physical world was designed and put together by the non-physical as already explained. The intricate details, the intent and the laws that ensure everything operates in harmony are the clear fingerprints of the Designer, Creator. He is more real scientifically/ logically than you reading this – you didn't create yourself, the laws that govern your body, the choice to reason. Even the very thing that you use or create is developed from the raw material and the laws He created. Do you give Him thanks or yourself? Who is the one who is prideful? Who is honoured - The house (the body) or the one living in the house (Self) or the Creator (God) who built the house and everything around it?

You need to be against God to miss the details of life. You might as well say that the stars are disappearing. If they are disappearing is it not modern pollution that stops us from seeing them? Is this not the price we pay in our great cities; lots of pollution, lots of lamps, but no stars? Doesn't mean they are not there. Similarly, the world is self focused and is opposed to God, except itself being god with quotes like "believe in yourself" concepts. Are not most of our television programs, educational system, our radio stations and books biased away from God and towards self? Putting obstacles in our way to prevent us from seeing God?

You think you are a genius for not believing in God? You are no genius but a product of your environment. How can you be open-minded/ a free thinker when your eyes are covered by the obvious? It is more acceptable to the world and less confrontational to deny God than to accept Him. In this world those who surrender to God are wise and courageous; those who reject Him are fools and cowards. He is watching what we do with the freewill He gave us. Do we grope for Him or self?

Have I ruffled your feathers – I meant to provoke you to think twice, to think logically and not what someone tells you. Have you really thought about life, or taken on what others have said about life, without challenging those ideas and made them your own? Have you professed that they are your own ideas or acknowledged that they are someone else's? From very young we believe in a Creator, Some Designer, God, but over time due to false education, false motives, self focus, we are brainwashed not to believe in Him. So if anything we are more programmed "not" to believe He is than to believe.

Most people only break through the calamity of doubt and sin when a hopeless situation hits them and they grope for God through prayer. Why? Is it because deep down they know He is there and know He is their final hope? Why didn't they seek Him earlier? I must confess I was like this for nearly 24 years of my life. Don't laugh at me, God has probably been trying to reach you for years too and unless you repent you will perish in yourself.

I hear some say - "Why doesn't God just show Himself physically then I will believe?" There are two ways of answering this:

1. He has, through His Son over 2,000 years ago and raised Him from the dead but you don't believe it because you probably don't believe the Bible or look at History. If I had the time I would cross reference the Bible with archeology, science,

geology, history and the many non-biblical sources that talk about the man Jesus and the impact He had on many. Whatever you believe you need to wrestle with "who is Jesus", there is no one in history who was more influential than Him. Even when most people write down the date they are referencing Jesus' birth (e.g. 2000AD). So who is Jesus to you – His main message was either a lie, crazy or who He said He was. He didn't leave the option open for being just a good guy or a good prophet. His main message was that He is the Son of God and that He alone is the ONLY way to God the Father. Not only for those people in His day on earth but for all ages. And if they don't believe in Him they will continue to die in their sins. So who is Jesus to you – a liar, lunatic or who He said He was?

I hear some say, "Why didn't He come earlier, just after Adam and Eve?" Would the answer truly make any difference in your decision? However one of the many reasons He came when He did was to help people to believe Him. He fulfilled prophecies concerning Himself that were written 400-1000+ years earlier, one of the many ways He proved who He was. He also came proclaiming the Kingdom of God during the second evil empire to show the contrast between the Kingdom of the world and the Kingdom of God.

Or "what about those who don't know about Jesus?" God continues to show Himself through His creation, through reasoning, by their conscience, by love and through faith which all live by. They still need to grope for Him, call out for Him. And God will be more tolerant towards them on Judgment Day than those who have heard about Jesus as the way of life and rejected Him.

2. "Why doesn't God show Himself <u>continually</u>, so we can see Him physically when we want to?" Now honestly speaking, if you saw God continually, would you follow Him - honestly? Don't say yes hastily, Adam and Eve walked with God and chose to disobey. Adam's motivation for eating the forbidden fruit of the knowledge of good and evil was "wanting to be like God", a god unto himself. He wanted to be governed by his own rules and not God's rules – sound familiar? For we have all sinned and fallen short before the

presence of God, it is in our genes through Adam and self. That's why we need His help and He provided it by sending us His Son. His Son paid for the sins of those who come to Him. And they will only come to Him when they humble themselves.

God is in the process of selecting those who are worthy to be with Him, based on their choice in choosing Him. It is not based on their choice of what they call "being good". They are not good – for all have sinned, all have lied, all have stolen, all have rebelled against God – yet they call themselves good because they haven't murdered anyone. It is about acknowledging our fallen nature by choosing His Son.

Can you imagine spending "eternity" with people who will grow to despise you and you can do nothing about it? What would be better - to get rid of them upfront or let them infect the people who love you like bad apples? How would you select the right people through the centuries...?

Is there any better test than to give them the "ability" to reason you without seeing you? The ability to reason life and love, the "ability" to listen to you (conscience). And if they reason and listen to you without seeing you physically, when the entire world is pushing them away from you, how much MORE will they want to be with you when they see you? Similarly if we love God now, how much more will we when we physically see Him. Is there any better test for eternal loyalty than to give the freedom of choice to choose Him and then watch what people do with that choice - Use it or abuse it? Will they embrace His authority over them or reject Him? Their words and deeds speak. In this world not everyone are His children, only those who love Him and surrender their will to His Son, Jesus Christ, are His Children (John 1:12).

Chapter 5

Have you challenged your base?

For those who remain blind to the evidence provided – I challenge you before God to answer these 9 questions for yourself, can you stand?

1. What is your source and why do you trust it? Has your source ever been wrong?

2. How do you govern and differentiate what is good and evil, or right and wrong – Trace it back to the source - the Bible or …?

3. If everyone lived like you what would happen?

4. What is the meaning of life, and what is that based upon?

5. Do you have inner peace or a void?

6. What are the chances that there is no Creator who put life together (0-100%)? If anything less than 100% then why the doubt - Is it that you believe there is a Creator?

7. What more would God need to do in order to show you that Jesus is the One you need to surrender your life to in order to save you? "Why not ask Him and if you don't want to ask why not, what are you afraid of?"

8. Do you know who Jesus Christ of Nazareth is, what He did for you and your potential future?

9. When you die one day and stand before God what would you say to Him - when He asks you why you have rejected His Son?
    a. Would you blame Him for not showing Himself physically?

b. Blame Him for not making it clearer, by spelling it out in a book?
c. Challenge Him for His unfairness because you are more righteous and you know better?
d. Or...?

Chapter 6

Is the Bible LITERALLY God's Word?

The Bible is an extension of the Jewish Scriptures, talking about the Messiah. The question is - Do the books in the Bible claim to be the Word of God? Yes (2 Tim. 3:16; Matt. 5:17, 7:12; Luke 24:44). The words contained in these books are inspired by God Himself, and they are breathed out through mankind (2 Peter 1:21; 2 Sam. 23:2; Num. 22:35; Matt. 4:4). Did God speak directly through people that caused them to write, "Thus says the LORD"? The following logical facts prove that the Bible is the Word of God. Can any other book or authority match up? This question I will allow you to answer as you dwell on these facts.

i) **Any ancient historical sources saying the same thing?**

Generally people believe the explainable events in the Bible but not those that can't be explained by our understanding or science. They ignore the God factor and believe the book was written by man - if they believed God then it wouldn't be impossible for God to have done these things.

So let's first see if some of these so called "questionable events" like Creation, Noah and the flood, the Plagues in Egypt, are backed up in other external sources besides the Bible?

- The Creation account is also recorded in the Ebla Tablet (dating back to ~2,000BC), and specifically attributing creation to one great being "Lugal" literally meaning "the Great One."

- The flood that covered the entire earth (~2,350BC) is also mentioned as a "great flood that destroyed the world" in the "Sumerian Kings" (dating back to 2,000-2,250BC).

- The plagues God poured out on the Egyptians when He came against their gods are also recorded in the Egyptian Hieroglyphics "Ipuwer Papyrus" (dating back to ~1,450BC).

Also people in the Bible are verified through external historical documentation e.g. Roman emperors: Caesar Augustus, Tiberius, and Claudius. Roman governors: Pontius Pilate, Serguis Paulus, Gallio, Felix and Festus. Local rulers: Herod the Great, Archelaus, Herod Antipas, Philip, Herod Agrippa I, Herod Agrippa II, Lysanias and Aretas IV. High priests: Annas, Joseph Caiaphas and Ananias. Prominent women: Herodias, Salome, Bernice and Drusilla. And just recently archaeologists discovered the supposed bones of the chief prosecutor at that trial of Jesus, the high priest Joseph Caiaphas, inside an ossuary (a stone chest used to store bones from burial sites).

Flavius Josephus, a Jewish historian of the 1st Century, also wrote about Jesus and His impact (Antiquities 18:63-64), "At this time there was a wise man called Jesus, and his conduct was good, and he was known to be virtuous. Many people among the Jews and the other nations became his disciples. Pilate condemned him to be crucified, and to die. But those who had become his disciples did not abandon his discipleship. They reported that he had appeared to them three days after his crucifixion, and that he was alive. Accordingly, he was perhaps the Messiah (the Christ), concerning whom the prophets have reported wonders. And the tribe of the Christians, so named after him, has not disappeared to this day."

Also throughout history, Archaeologists continually use the Bible as a source to validate cities, towns, regions and authorities. These historical facts are undisputed.

ii) What are the amazing facts?

1. It is the only Book to originate in 3 languages, yet with a consistent message: Hebrew (most of the OT), Aramaic (Daniel 2-7, Ezra 4-7, Matt. 27:46) and Greek (most of the NT).

2. The books were written in different places – what is known today as Asia, Africa and Europe.

3. The time span from the first to the last writer is ~2,000years - no other book comes close.

4. The events described in the Bible range from just before 4,000BC to Eternity.

5. The Bible is the only Book that has been translated into more languages than any other. Most of the so-called "great" books have been translated into 5 languages but the Bible has been translated into ~2,200 languages, which reaches 90%+ of the world's population. Why is this important? This is further evidence that God wants people to know His Word.

6. The Bible is the only religious "Mainstream" book permitting the common man to have access to it. Again God wants all to know what He said.

7. After people were permitted to read the Bible in England, it was used to break literacy barriers.

8. The Bible has more critics than any other book ever written; yet it is the only book that silences these critics with facts.

9. The Bible is the only Book that world leaders have actually planned to exterminate, and the people who followed it. Antiochus IV Epiphanies (a Syrian leader) was determined to destroy Israel and burn all the Hebrew Scriptures. 2 centuries later (31-64AD), the Jewish leaders tried to exterminate the Christians. Gamaliel, who was a well respected Jewish teacher of the law at that time, stood up in the council at Jerusalem, saying in Acts 5:38-39, "And now I say to you, keep away from these men and let them alone; for if this plan or this work is of men, it will come to nothing; but if it is of God, you cannot overthrow it—lest you even be found to fight against God." His declaration had no impact and the persecution continued. Also the Roman Emperors tried to exterminate Christians and the Bible, the worst of them being Nero (54-68AD), Domitian (81-96AD), Decius (249-251AD) and Diocletian (284-305AD). More recently under Nazism, Communism, Islam, Hinduism, Buddhism, where the Bible & Christians are considered one of their biggest enemies. The Bible has surely stood the test of persecution.

10. It is the only "religious" Book that centers on God's love and His redemption plan for mankind, "Not leaving man in the deprived state of sin, but providing the way of escape" and says "God is love". The Bible also describes how to live life and express love. And all things that are important for making daily decisions – having a relationship with the Creator, marriage, parenting, sexuality, divorce, authorities, leadership, work ethics, what things to avoid, etc. Providing a moral compass that is life changing, the evidence of which fills our history books.

11. It is the only Book where the message came from God in many different forms - dreams, transportation, visions, revelations from Angels, messages by way of miracles, audible and inner voices, never contradicting the message in the Torah (1st 5 books of the Bible).

12. God revealed Himself to all through creation, but made His Character known through Israel. Jesus told the Samaritan woman, "You worship what you don't know, we (the Jews) know what we worship, for salvation is of the Jews. BUT

the hour is coming, and now is when the true worshippers will worship the Father in spirit and truth" (John 4:22-23). Jesus acknowledged that only the Jewish people had the ability to worship God. Why? Because God had given Israel His Word (the Hebrew Canon).

Why only Israel and not everyone? If you were God, how would you show who you were without physically showing yourself to everyone? You would select the weakest people on earth and then demonstrate your influence and power through them. Any nation who came against the nation you are helping would lose. This is what God did with Israel; He chose the weakest of people and with His Word and guidance made them strong. When other nations looked at Israel they said – How is this possible because they aren't the strongest, it must be the God whom they serve!

There are other so-called gods in the world (e.g. Satan, Self) but there is only one True God, the Creator and it is He who gave all freewill – to either choose Him or reject Him. God delivered the Israelites from Egypt and came against the 10 Egyptian gods whom they worshipped; neither the Egyptians nor their gods could face the God of Israel. The plagues did not touch the Israelites; it only came on the Egyptians. Now if you saw that distinction, what would you have thought? This is not only documented in the Bible but also in the Egyptian Hieroglyphics "Ipuwer Papyrus". What caused this? It was not the will of the Israelites, it was not the belief of the Egyptians nor was it a figment of their imagination; but it was God who said it would come and it did, on cue through the mouth of Moses.

Similarly, Elijah challenged the prophets of Baal to show them that their god would not be able to stand against God Almighty. After the prophets of Baal couldn't incite Baal, who they created, to bring fire down on the sacrifice, they gave up. The True God through Elijah sent fire to come down from Heaven and consume the water saturated sacrifice that Elijah had prepared. This was performed in front of many people, and more specifically in front of the 450 prophets of Baal. What would you have done if you were there? Continue serving Baal or follow the God of Elijah who is the God of Israel?

And today, there are many other examples, where people have been supernaturally healed of incurable diseases and raised from the dead, in the name of Jesus Christ, whose Father is the God of Israel.

iii) How do we know man didn't write the Bible to keep peace?

Some will say, "The Bible was written by man to ensure peace is maintained". This is illogical because if it was man focused it would be self-focused and not God focused. The reason this statement is made is because people don't want to be accountable to God. But if the statement comes from – If there is a Creator, God, I "would" want to know and I "will" follow Him, then allow me to answer this statement from a historical and philosophical perspective:

- The Bible is the only book where people speaking God's Word "were not" motivated by personal needs but to express exactly what God said because they feared God more than man. It is the only book where some of the prophets "were killed" when delivering the message of God. This is proof that the prophets feared God more than man, even to the point of death. What would make you tell people the message of God even if you knew they would kill you? If God, or an Angel, or a strong inner conviction told you?

- Another view - If it was man motivated - the concept of love would have been as a reward and not as a first effort. God says you love Me and others, and you will be blessed. Man says I need to be blessed first and then I will love. Man says get even, but Jesus said in Matt. 5:44, "I say to you, love your enemies, bless those who curse you, do good to those who hate you, and pray for those who spitefully use you and persecute you." Does this honestly sound man motivated?

- Another view - Man would not have condemned themselves as sinners unless truth existed in the first place. When mankind is compared to the 10 commandments he fails on every account; all have rebelled against God, all have lied, all have stolen, and the list goes on.

- Another view - When people sin they receive the consequences of emptiness, guilt and depression. Why do they feel this if they don't know or believe His word? Their rebellion against God's Word screams on the inside of them, their conscience. They may silence their conscience but deep down they know they have sinned or are sinning.

- Another view - We know that people who make laws don't need to keep them because they are above the law they make e.g. the Government, Pharaoh, Kings or Queens. However the writers in the Bible were conformed to the word that they shared, even to the point of their death.

- Another view - If the Bible was written as an incentive for people to conform then all it would be are empty words with no backing, no benefits and no consequences. So why are people suffering today - Do you know? The Bible explains why people suffer and why they are blessed. It isn't by chance. Yes some good people suffer at the hands of evil people, and yes some who make millions are still miserable and doing everything to fill the void. The Bible explains this too. When people follow God's Word, good things start to happen.

As Peter said in 2 Peter 1:20-21 "knowing this first, that no prophecy of Scripture is of any private interpretation, for prophecy never came by the will of man, but holy men of God spoke as they were moved by the Holy Spirit."

iv) What are the main messages and themes in the Bible?

1. The Bible is the only Book to describe "how" to experience and express love, which is the meaning of life: 1) God's Love for us, 2) Love God, 3) Love Self, 4) Love other Christians more than self and 5) Love others like self. It is no coincidence that Christ's followers show love beyond anyone else. Not because they can in their own strength, but because they rely on Him. If they surrender to Him, then it is His love working through them. The more intimate the relationship they have with their Heavenly Father, who

is God, the more His love will rub off on them. For God is love (1 John 4:8). Jesus taught unconditional love - in Matt. 5:44-46, "I say to you, love your enemies, bless those who curse you, do good to those who hate you, and pray for those who spitefully use you and persecute you, that you may be sons of your Father in heaven; for He makes His sun rise on the evil and on the good, and sends rain on the just and on the unjust. For if you love those who love you, what reward have you? Do not even the tax collectors do the same?" A pretty high standard of love isn't it!

Now thinking logically, I put all the founders and religions on the table to see which one expresses the most love. For it is the expression of love which is the meaning of life, not in words but in deeds. Who gives up their life to love and help others? And whose house would I want to live in if I were ever handicapped, blind, an orphan or in need? How would they care for me? How would they treat me if I were a woman? These appear to be simple questions... I was surprised at how many fell by the way side after the very first question. Don't be deceived by "all religions are the same." They are not, don't be ignorant, check them out on these simple questions. I used to say all religions were the same until I did this simple exercise for myself.

It was Christians who started hospitals, orphanages, feeding those starving in Africa, clothing those in need, helping those who can't fend for themselves, like World Vision; started educational institutions to help educate those who can't afford it, they built and developed schools for the handicapped. Christians continue to be generous, out giving non-Christians 10 to 1 (look at the government records), and who continually will sacrifice themselves to go to hostile areas to teach God's love through missions. Many giving up their lives sacrificially to help those who end up killing them – even today. Some may say, "What about the Crusades?" What about them – they killed Christians and non Christians. Measure a Christian with respect to their founder not based on the title they give themselves. Also never think a Christian doesn't make mistakes. The reason they are Christians is because they "acknowledge" their mistakes and humble themselves under Christ's rule. So that Christ can work through them. The above examples are clear evidence of Him shining through them. But the question I would ask you - What will make you go beyond the safety of your comfort zones to help others you don't know or hate you? This is what Christians try to do in Him. Is there any greater love?

2. The Bible is the only Book to describe the 4 pillars of life:

- Our origin before we were born
- Our destination after we die
- The meaning of life
- The moral compass that is life changing

3. The main message of the Bible is God's love for us. And because He is a just and holy God, He will punish sin. Therefore because of His love, He sent His Son, Jesus the Messiah (the Christ). Jesus paid the price for the sins, i.e. paid for our rebellion against God with His own blood. Today the freedom that we experience in our country, with others, was due to the shedding

of blood of those who came before us. Freedom is not free! They paid for this freedom with their own blood. Without bloodshed there was no freedom. Similarly Jesus Christ shed His "sinless" blood so that we can have freedom with God. He gives eternal life to those who come to Him. It is not enough to believe in God. "You believe that there is one God; you do well even the demons believe and tremble" (James 2:19). But they aren't going to Heaven. God made the rules to get to Heaven, just like He made the rules for creation and everything in it. If we jump off a building because we don't want to believe in gravity, guess what happens? So why would we expect to get to Heaven without following the rules to get there?

Believing in God is not enough and what we call "good" makes no difference to what God calls good. And all our "so called" good works are filthy rags before Him (Isaiah 64:6), we are not God. His plan points to His Son, Jesus the Christ and the need to surrender to His Son. "God demonstrates His own love to us, while we being still sinners, Christ died <u>for us</u>" (Rom. 5:8).

And in John 3:16-18 "For God so loved the world insomuch that He gave His only born Son, so that whoever believes into Him should not perish but have everlasting life. For indeed God sent not His Son into the world in order to condemn the world, but in order that the world through Him be saved. He who believes into Him is not condemned, but he who believes not is condemned already, because he does not believe into the name of the only born Son of God". Jesus said, "No one can come to the Father except through ME" (John 14:6).

So it comes down to - You either believe Jesus was a liar or who He said He was. You can't play games with the fact He was just a good man. He didn't leave that option open. The Bible provides no alternatives but...... an ultimatum! The time is now, and everyone is responsible to choose God's Plan – i.e. surrender to His Son and be saved for eternity, or not and continue in eternal destruction. The choice is yours. This is the main message of the Bible.

v) **How do we know the writers were inspired by God?**

1. The ultimate truth test is putting God's Word into practice and you will start seeing things fall into place. It isn't a coincidence. What gives one nation more strength than another? It is not money or military might but wisdom. Wisdom is not knowing everything but knowing the right thing at the right time to implement it. It is the fear of the God of Israel, the Father of Christ, that brings wisdom, and when we fear God then we surrender to His Son – Jesus Christ.

    In the Bible there were many situations where the odds were against God's people but yet they were victorious. For example, Abraham destroyed those who came against him, armies much greater than his own. In fact, Abraham's household were just farmers who defeated experienced warriors. Moses destroyed most of Egypt and the Egyptians even though he and the Israelites didn't even lift a finger to fight against them. God fought on their behalf. Time fails to mention David, Solomon, Gideon, Asa, and Joshua - all of these men fought armies 10 to 100 times more in number, equipment and experience than them. Sometimes they just came around the corner and their enemies were already dead. When Israel turned away from God to follow their own wisdom (influenced by the nations around them and their own intellect) in ~700BC, then other nations and kingdoms possessed them until 1948AD. And today 5% of the world's population controls the rest – it has been like this for the last 1,700 years. When the authority of the country is founded on Jesus Christ then the land is blessed by God. God said choose life or death, blessings or curses, that is, choose His Son or not, the choice is yours (Deut. 28). Psalm 2:12 says, "Kiss the Son, lest He be angry, and you perish in the way, when His wrath is kindled but a little. Blessed are all those who put their trust in Him."

Some nations are clearly more blessed than others and others look cursed (don't just look at money) – look at what they believe and compare the authorities of the land to the scripture. Most of the nations that are blessed or were blessed based their authority on Christian principles (God's Word – the Bible). Also in God's Mercy, He allows His Children (Christians) to be persecuted by others in order to win the persecutors to Him. Many persecutors have given their life over to Jesus Christ because of the love, forgiveness and faith they saw in the very people they were persecuting. Again it is people who are doing the persecuting and not God. God doesn't change people's will but calls them to Him.

2. When the writers wrote "Thus says the Lord...." they never contradicted each other even when many of them hadn't met each other, nor had read what the others had written. It is impossible by human intervention, thus it was only possible because it was inspired by God. God cannot err (Titus 1:2; Heb. 6:18). There is not a book in the world with this level of complexity, level of diversity and yet with the same consistent message. Consider the following:

- The Bible was written by more than 40 writers, who came from every walk of life: fishermen, kings, philosophers, tax collectors, poets, musicians, statesmen, scholars, priests, shepherds, etc.; AND

- Written in many different styles – songs, parables, narrative, legal, poetic, historic, romantic, biographic, autobiographic, prophetic, satiric and allegoric; AND

- Written during the largest spectrum of circumstances and emotions; joy, war, sacrifice, famine, prosperity, conviction, persecution, yet the message stays consistent and without contradiction. It has been proven time and again that the only contradiction has been found in one's understanding.

3. Science confirms today what the Bible has said for thousands of years. What more will they confirm in the next few years? The question that should be asked is - how did they know the following facts back then when only now we have scientific evidence as proof? Only one answer - God inspired them! Here are some of those scientific statements God's Word makes:

- Many people in the ancient world, famous Greek philosophers, and religions believed that the earth was flat, never-ending, and some in the East believed it sat on a giant or an animal, but Isaiah (in the Bible Isaiah 40:22) spoke of the earth being a sphere in ~700BC, also Job 1,200 years earlier said that the earth hung upon nothing (Job 26:7 ~1900BC) and Jesus in ~30AD implied that the earth revolved so that at the same time there is day and night (Luke 17:34–36). Pretty amazing that science could only prove this 1000s of years later.

- God's Word tells us that the earth was split apart after the flood ~2,300BC (1 Chr. 1:19). Science only in the last few centuries was able to prove that the earth, at one point, was a large mass that split apart. The difference between the Bible and soft science is timing of when it happened. Another amazing fact.

- God told us what were good meats to eat (Deut. 14 ~1,400BC) - Good meats to eat are sheep, cattle, goats, chickens and bad meats are pork, shell fish, cats, dogs, snakes etc. Science recently released that these bad meats are filled with toxins and harmful to us.

- Jesus told those who believe, that in the name of Jesus Christ they are to lay hands on the sick and the sick will recover (Mark 16:19 ~31AD). Many are healed in the name of Jesus, where some doctors attribute it to a positive environment but yet they can't reproduce it because they are missing the key – Jesus Christ.

- God's Word says a merry heart is like good medicine (Prov. 17:22 ~800BC), science confirms that a merry heart improves health.

- God's Word has said from the beginning that the physical world is made up of the invisible (Gen. 1:1-26 written ~1,450BC, and Heb. 11:3 in ~60AD), only in the 20th Century have scientists proven that the world is made up of the invisible – variation of energy. Thus nothing is solid and everything is just a variation of energy. Bible had been saying this 1000s of years earlier.

4. The Bible is the only Book to be copied many times on perishables like animal skin and papyrus (sometimes on stone, wood, clay), yet it still maintained its integrity and its accuracy. Think of the impossibility of this happening when we know that the Bible is the most copied Book in History. So how do we know it is accurate?

- Comparing OT Ancient Text such as the Dead Sea scrolls (200BC-68AD) to the latest Hebrew Text which is used for translation such as Ben Chayyim (1525AD) and the Leningrad Codex (1008AD). The accuracy over 1,500 years is astounding, unparalleled and frankly beyond amazing. Although vowels were later added to the Hebrew Text; the sequence of events and words remained exactly the same. There have been a few interpretation/translation discrepancies from the original language into other languages but the original language still remains unparalleled in accuracy. What was the motivation behind people copying them so accurately? God, His Word is a love song with personal direction similar to a musical piece; alter one note and you change the song. This is why God warns people not to take away or add to His Word, actually He forbids it and there are consequences for those who do (Deut. 4:2; Prov. 30:5, 6; Rev. 22:18).

- The manuscript evidence for the NT is also dramatic, with over 5,300 known copies and fragments in the original Greek, nearly 800 of which were copied before 1,000AD. Some manuscript texts such as the Aramaic Text date as early as 130-150AD. Less than 80 years after the original writings (50-95AD) known as autographs. Interestingly, these manuscripts surpass the reliability of all the other ancient writings put together. Many historians trust ancient literature as reliable and authentic but compared to the NT they don't even come close.

5. The Bible contains many prophecies that have been fulfilled, and some still to come. Here is

one of the macro prophecies written before they came to pass:

- The rise and fall of the 5 EVIL Empires/Kingdoms before Christ comes to reign over the earth. Daniel had been given the prophecies of the last 5 Evil Empires that God would allow to rule over His people. Why would God allow His people to be ruled by Evil? Because of their rebellion against Him. Now when Daniel (~600BC) prophesied (Dan. 2:14-45), he was in one Evil Empire and four had not yet come. Babylon 606BC (Dan. 1:1), Media-Persia 536BC (Dan. 5:28; 8:20; 9:24); Greece 336BC (Dan. 8:21; 10:20), the Roman Empire (Dan. 9:25), and one is yet to come. Except for the last one which has not come, both history and external sources have confirmed what Daniel had prophesied many years earlier – how these Empires would rise and how they would fall.

For those who are interested in the final Evil Empire that would come before Jesus physically reigns on earth – here are 4 signs for you from the Bible. The purpose of the prophecies isn't just for you to know but for you to do something about it.

a) The final Evil Empire consists of 10 nations (Dan. 7:7; 2:41-42; Rev. 13:1) and is located on the 7 heads, i.e. "7 mountains" (Rev. 17:9 – Rome was known to be the seat of the seven hills). It is similar to the previous Evil Empires (Rev. 17:10), but will be more like the Old Roman Empire (a larger version of the EU today). This empire will be ruled by 10 leaders the Bible calls kings. They will have blasphemous names, probably something like what the Roman emperors in the 1st and 2nd Century had on their heads "Theos" meaning god, implying they are the world's god (Rev. 17:3). This empire will be partly strong and partly fragile symbolised by the Iron and Clay feet, also it is more balanced than the previous Empires, symbolized by "toes" and a "balance between the strong iron for tension and clay strong for compression" (Dan. 2:33, 41-43). The strongest 3 of the 10 kings will be clearly uprooted by a man the Bible calls "the Beast", also known as Gog. He will probably be a descendant of Japheth because he is of the land of Magog (Gen. 10:2) and from the region far north of Israel (Ezek. 38:15; 39:1-2) therefore probably a Caucasian or Asian. He comes from amongst the 3 strongest kings and suppresses them (Dan. 7:20, 23-24) thus becoming ruler over all 10 kings and speaking on their behalf (Dan. 7:7-8, 20, 23-24; Rev. 17:11, 13).

He initiates and gets the world to sign a peace treaty with Israel for 7 years. Because of this, he is seen as a hero and they celebrate this peace, which is a false "peace" (Dan. 9:27; 1 Thess. 5:3). He will speak what people want to hear - speaking to their lusts (Dan. 7:8). He will proclaim inclusion of all and those of the world will be quick to embrace him. But it will also be hypocritical as he will try to abolish God's Laws and re-establish his own laws for people to follow. He will write his own book of laws for people to follow; trying to be a god to all. Now just before God removes Christians from the earth, he will be mortally wounded by a sword/knife, which will be noticeable by all, like a beheading or something just as drastic. But he will be brought back to life by Satan who incarnates him "giving him his power", this is after Satan is kicked out of Heaven forever (Dan. 11:45; Rev. 12:9, 12; 13:12, 14; 17:11). People will be in awe at what just happened, and he will declare that he is the Messiah the prophets spoke about.

b) The general world culture leading up to the Evil Empire described in 2 Tim. 3:1-5, "People will be lovers of themselves, lovers of money, boasters, proud, blasphemers, disobedient to parents, unthankful, unholy, unloving, unforgiving, slanderers, without self-control, brutal, despisers of good, traitors, headstrong, haughty, lovers of pleasure rather than lovers of God, having a form of godliness but denying its power." And Peter expresses in 2 Peter 3:3-6 that there will be many scoffers who will mock God's Word and Christians. They will find ways to escape reality by getting drunk, drugged, self-meditation, and thereby ignoring the reality of eternity and repentance towards God.

c) Signs of the world and earth leading up to the Evil Empire: Jesus said in Matt. 24, Mark 13, Luke 21; "Now when you will hear of wars and reports of wars and instability, watch not the trouble. Be not startled, for indeed all these must first come to pass but immediately the end is not yet. For indeed nation will rise against nation, and Kingdom against Kingdom. And there will be great earthquakes in various places, and there will be famines and troubles and pestilences. Now all these are the beginnings …".

d) Signs of the time leading up to the Evil Empire: Counting from when Adam and Eve were created until the start of the world's tribulation period is 5,993 years. Why 5,993 years? Because at the 6,000 year mark Christ reigns for 1,000 years (the earth's Sabbath). And just before His reign the world experiences the wrath of Christ and of God for 7 years. So where are we in terms of the

Biblical timeline? We don't exactly know the day or the hour but we have a 100 year range - Based on Biblical chronology we know as of 2010 it is ~5960 years since Adam and Eve were created – therefore the mid point would be 2043AD, but it can be anytime before or anytime after. So what is the principle? Be ready!

6. Lastly, Jesus Christ of Nazareth Himself is the evidence – The question everyone is faced with is - Do I believe Him or not? If I do, then the Bible is God's Word.

Chapter 7

Is Jesus the Messiah, the One we are to SURRENDER to?

- **3 Years.** Jesus ministered for only 3 years and made the biggest impact the world has ever seen or known. Even the dating of our years is based on His birth (BC & AD). For the good news of Jesus Christ to spread across the world like it has must have been divinely inspired. No other comes close.

- **Miracles.** Jesus performed miracles that no one ever did. How do we know He performed the miracles? What would cause people who were steeped in their Jewish tradition to change and be convinced that these miracles were from God? The miracles would need to be impossible and have lasting results. People were in awe and made statements like, "Will the Christ do more signs than this man has done?" (John 7:31). Also if we were in a court of law and we had 2 witnesses describing the same events, then their testimony would be considered true if they matched. How much more accurate when we have 4 witnesses; Matthew, Mark, Luke and John, who feared God, who wrote these in different places and from different angles, and all say the same thing. The question is what would Jesus need to do, in order to prove that He was the Son of God to you, and this proof would result in you laying down your life in sharing the good news concerning Him?" Well this is the question many 1st Century people experienced, which resulted in them giving up their life to tell others. They saw Jesus heal the sick; He raised the dead; He walked on water; He commanded the storm to cease and it did; He spoke about the future which came to pass, He fed over 5,000 people with 5 loaves and 2 fish until they were all filled; He commanded evil spirits to leave and they did; He made the blind see and the deaf hear; He spoke with Angels; He spoke with Moses and

Elijah who had died centuries earlier; He healed the lame and they walked; He made those who were missing body parts whole; He commanded the fish into the nets; He resurrected Himself from the dead after 3 days, then He ascended to Heaven in front of them. What would you have done if you saw this? Would you have given your life over, really?

- **Resurrection.** We can dig up the bones and visit the burial sites of all the founders of the different religions, except for Jesus Christ who has risen. No other religion claims that their founder is still alive except Christians. No other religion has ever seen their founder physically after the founder died except the Christians.

- **Fulfilled Prophecy.** As mathematicians, I ask you to look at the evidence and calculate the probability that Jesus of Nazareth is the Messiah (the Christ); by the fact He fulfilled scripture from 1,400 to 400 years "before" He was born in flesh. This Jesus is the same Messiah that God told Moses would come (Deut. 8:18-19), "I will raise up for them a Prophet like you from among their brethren, and will put My words in His mouth, and He shall speak to them all that I command Him. And it shall be that whoever will not hear My words, which "He speaks" in My name, I will require it of him." There is more than 1×10^{18} probability that Jesus is the Messiah prophesied about in the scripture. I bank my entire life on these kinds of odds and so should you. This is a "very" conservative as it ignores 100's of prophecies and all major prophecies e.g. the virgin birth of Jesus Christ; John the Baptist born of a woman past menopause; healing the deaf, the blind and lame; He being sold for 30 pieces of silver and the money later used to purchase the potter's field; being resurrected in a physical body. These prophecies would turn the probability to infinity.

Let me share the method of calculating probability: If we were going to drive downtown and there were 10 traffic lights - what is the probability of them all turning green without us having to slow down? Assuming they only have red and green lights (amber is insignificant relative to time) AND the time they change is equal to one another. So for each traffic light, we have 1 in 2 odds of passing through it green. Therefore the probability would look like 1/2 x 1/2 x 1/2 x 1/2 x 1/2 x 1/2 x 1/2 x 1/2 x 1/2 x 1/2 that is 1/1024, same as a 1 in 1,024 probability of passing the 10 lights all green without slowing down. Or said another way, 1,024 probability of NOT passing all the green lights without slowing down. So based on the same methodology let's take a few of these prophecies concerning Jesus Christ fulfilling the conditions of the Messiah (the King of the earth, Son of God, the One who God told us to obey). And let's break it down into two main areas – 1) paternal lineage through which He came and 2) what happened to Him once He was on earth:

1. Establishing the paternal lineage relative to the population (assuming males were 50% of the population). The probability that Jesus fulfilled the conditions of the Messiah is 1×10^{12}, based on:

    - 1 in 20,000 to 350,000 odds - Jesus specifically is the seed of Abraham (Gen. 22:18; Matt. 1:1, 17). Population at that time was anywhere from 40,000 to 700,000 people.

- 1 in 2+ odds – Jesus' lineage is through Isaac and not Ishmael (Gen. 21:12; 26:2-4; Matt. 1:2).

- 1 in 2 odds – Jesus' lineage is through Jacob (Gen. 28:13-14; Num. 24:17, 19; Matt. 1:2). Jacob being 1 of the 2 sons of Isaac.

- 1 in 12 odds – Jesus' lineage is through Judah (Gen. 49:10; Micah 5:2; Matt. 1:2). Judah being 1 of the 12 sons of Jacob.

- 1 in 8 odds – Jesus' lineage is through King David (1 Sam. 16:1; 2 Sam. 7:12-14; Matt. 1:6). David being 1 of the 8 sons of Jesse.

- 1 in 140,000 to 280,000 odds - Jesus would be born in Bethlehem (Micah 5:2; Matt. 2:1-6). Jesus being one of 140,000 to 280,000 men born in Bethlehem, from Micah until He was born (~700 years). Those in Bethlehem were predominantly of those born through the lineage of David.

2. What happened to Him once He was on earth - The probability that Jesus fulfilled the conditions of the Messiah is 1×10^6, based on:

- Wise men from the east told Herod the Great that the Messiah was born. And it was the Jewish Rabbi's who shared the prophecy with Herod of where the Messiah would be born, Bethlehem. Herod was compelled to kill all male children in Bethlehem from 2 years old and under, at the same time Jesus was born (Jer. 31:15; Matt. 2:17-18). What would compel Herod the Great to do such a thing in Bethlehem unless he believed it to be true OR believed that the people believed this to be true and wanted to stop their belief? Either case there are so many ways of evaluating the probability of this from Bethlehem being 1 in 60+ cities under his jurisdiction plus 1 in 10+ ways Herod would respond to it, so I will not include it in the probability calculation.

- 1 in 2 odds - Jesus was called out of Egypt to Israel (Hos. 11:1; Matt. 2:14-15; 19-21). Joseph having 1 of 2 options, either to stay in Herod's jurisdiction or flee to Egypt which was under Rome's jurisdiction. Once Herod died they returned from Egypt to Israel.

- 1 in 2 odds – Israel leaders chose to reject Jesus (Ps. 35:19; Is. 53:1-3; John 1:11). They either accepted Him or rejected Him; His message of being the only Son of God was too drastic for them to be on the fence.

- 1 in 12 odds - Jesus would be betrayed by His friend, Judas (Ps. 41:9; John 17:12). Judas was 1 of his 12 disciples, whom Jesus knew about but allowed in order to fulfill scripture.

- 1 in 4 odds - Jesus was betrayed by Judas for exactly 30 pieces of silver and this money was later used to purchase the potters field (Zech. 11:12-14; Matt. 27:1-10). The decision was agreed upon by 2 parties - the priests and Judas. The probability of exactly "30 pieces" and of "silver" and then the money used specifically to purchase "the potter's field" is 1 in near 1,000,000+ odds, so I will leave this out in the calculation and just use the choice to make the decision 1 in 4 odds.

- 1 in 8 odds - Jesus was flogged and beaten and spat upon (Is. 50:6; Matt. 26:67; 27:26-30).

- 1 in 96 odds - Jesus was mocked, His hands and feet were pierced, He was crucified (Ps. 22:7-8, 16; Zech. 12:10; John 19:37). Decision not to stone Jesus as the Jewish custom but handed Him over to the Romans, they chose crucifixion by piercing both His Hands + his feet + pierced his side (they rarely pierced those crucified, they normally broke their legs and they died by suffocation. They pierced Him to confirm He was dead).

- 1 in 2 odds – Soldiers gambled for Jesus' clothes (Ps. 22:18; Matt. 27:35), a choice they made.

- 1 in 4 odds - Jesus was buried in a rich man's grave (Is. 53:9; Matt. 27:57-60). The Rich man chose to take Jesus knowing he would be ostracized by the Jewish leaders. He built the tomb for himself and gave his own tomb to Jesus as he considered Jesus being more valuable than himself.

By combining these prophecies of 1) & 2) we have more than 1×10^{18} probability that Jesus fulfilled the conditions of the Messiah. These prophecies were all made long before Christ arrived in flesh. There are 100's more prophecies that I could add but the above already is beyond anything we currently bank our life on. In fact, the probability that you will eat your next meal before you die is significantly becoming less and less, far less than what Christ offers you today.

- **In closing** - Jesus confronted those who did not believe that He was the Messiah (John 5:38-40, 46-47; John 14:6), "You do not have God's word abiding in you, because whom He sent, Him you do not believe. You search the Scriptures, for in them you think you have eternal life; and these are they which testify of Me. But you are not willing to come to Me that you may have life.... For if you believed Moses, you would believe Me;

for he wrote about Me. But if you do not believe his writings, how will you believe My words?"... "I am the way, the truth and the life: no man comes to the Father except through me".

If you don't believe and you die, it will be too late. Neither wisdom, money, self-righteousness, psychology, negotiation skills, nor religion can save you from eternal destruction, only Jesus can because He paid the price. This is the reason God sent Him - to make a way of escape for us, and to make a way for us to have an intimate relationship with Him for eternity, starting now. Jesus said (Matt. 16:26), "For what profit is it to a man if he gains the whole world, and loses his own soul? Or what will a man give in exchange for his soul?"

(Luke 16:19-31 extract from the Holy Gospels in One), "Now there was a certain wealthy man who also wore purple and fine linen. Being merry in luxury every day. Now there was a certain beggar named Lazarus, who was brought unto his gateway, full of sores and desiring to be satisfied from the crumbs falling away from the rich one's table. But even the dogs coming to lick his sores. And it came to pass that the beggar died, and he was carried away by the angels into Abraham's bosom. Now the wealthy one also died and was buried. And in Hades he lifted up his eyes, being in torments. Seeing Abraham away from afar and Lazarus in his bosom. And he called for him, saying, "Father Abraham, have mercy on me and send Lazarus so that he dip the tip of his finger in water and cool my tongue, because I am in agony in this same flame." Now Abraham said, "Child, remember that you in your life received good things and likewise Lazarus evil things. Now this moment this one here is comforted, now you are in agony. And besides all these, between us and you there is a great chasm established, so that they desiring to step over from here unto you cannot, nor cross over unto us from there." Now he said, "I ask you therefore father, so that you send him to my father's house, for indeed I have five brothers, so that he earnestly testify to them lest they also come into this place of torment." Abraham said to him, "They have Moses and the prophets, hear them." Now he said, "No indeed Father Abraham, but if one should go unto them away from the dead, they will repent." Now he said to him, "If they do not hear Moses and the prophets, neither would they be persuaded if a certain one rose from the dead."

Is this you? Here is the key – it's your choice. Repent and as Paul said (Rom. 10:9-13), "if you confess with your mouth the Lord Jesus and believe in your heart that God has raised Him from the dead, you will be saved. For with the heart one believes unto righteousness, and with the mouth confession is made unto salvation. For the Scripture says, "WHOEVER BELIEVES ON HIM WILL NOT BE PUT TO SHAME." For there is no distinction between Jew and Greek, for the same Lord over all is rich to all who call upon Him. For "WHOEVER CALLS ON THE NAME OF THE LORD SHALL BE SAVED." Jesus said, "Behold, I stand at the door and knock. If anyone hears My voice and opens the door, I will come in to him and dine with him, and he with Me" (Rev 3:20).

LaVergne, TN USA
13 May 2010
182656LV00001B/2/P